P.S. I Love You

by Will Bullas

*to Scott, Patty,
Happy 16th
Anniversary !
Our Love Forever,
Phil + Flaa*

lovey dovey...

THE GREENWICH WORKSHOP PRESS

A GREENWICH WORKSHOP PRESS BOOK

Copyright ©2001 by The Greenwich Workshop Press
All art ©Will Bullas

Published by the Greenwich Workshop Press. One Greenwich Place, P.O. Box 875, Shelton, CT 06484. (203) 925-0131 or (800) 243-4246.

Library of Congress Cataloging-in-Publication Data
Bullas, Will, 1949-
      P.S. I love you / by Will Bullas
         p. cm.
ISBN 0-86713-071-7 (alk. paper)
      1. Bullas, Will, 1949- 2. Love in art. 3. Animals in art. 4. American wit and humor,
Pictorial. I. Title

ND1839.B77 A4 2001a
759.13--dc21

2001040307

Limited edition prints and canvas reproductions, and figurines based on Will Bullas' paintings, are available exclusively through The Greenwich Workshop, Inc. and its 1200 dealers in North America. Collectors interested in obtaining information on available releases and the location of their nearest dealer are requested to visit our website at **www.greenwichworkshop.com** or to write or call the publisher at the address above.

Jacket front: *puppy lover...*
Book design by Sheryl P. Kober
Printed in Singapore by Imago
First Printing 2001
1 2 3 4 5   04 03 02 01

The Art of Love

Will Bullas fires Cupid's arrow in these positively beastly accounts of the complexities of love. No species is immune to the lovebug's bite, and these creatures have all caught some rather human emotions. Prepare yourself for antic artistry and take a look at love through the eyes of the animals that skulk, waddle and leap out of the pages of this animated love letter. From the lovelorn giraffes that have to endure *long distance love*… to the smooth-talking frog who claims he's *toadally yours*… love is even more universal than you think.

toadally yours...

honey bun...

big hearted..

*a whole
lotta love...*

long distance love affair...

o horney devil...

please bee mine...

the drive-in...

pig 'o my heart...

a hop, a skip and a smooch...

ducky in love.

leaper's love...

I remembered the big box...

a visit from the in-laws...

*Faithful
companions...*

honeybuns...

art

from

the

heart...

romancing the monkey...

3-d double creature feature...

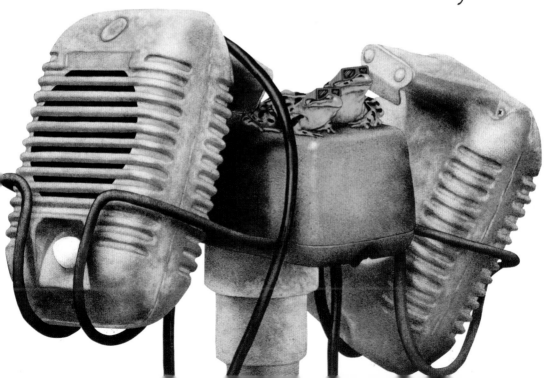

p.s. I love you...

pugs
and
kisses...

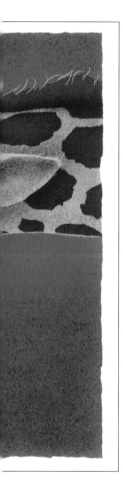

lofty lovers...

let it be a dance...

southern belles...

puppy lover...

sweets...

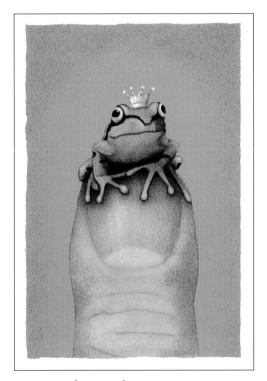

thumbprints...

althea...

lovers leap...

chicks and cheap wine...

hot chicks in high heels...

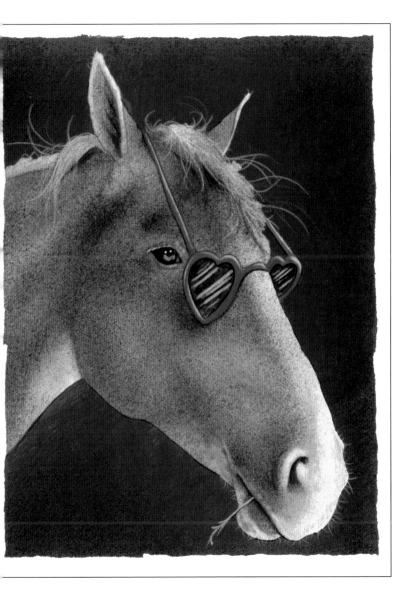

horse lover...

autumn romance...